CITIES AT WAR

Robin Cross

Wayland

CITIES AT WAR

Other titles in this series:

Aftermath of War
Children and War
Propaganda
Technology of War
Victims of War
Women and War
World Leaders

Cover illustration: A worker stands in front of the skyline of a blazing city. Huge bombing attacks levelled parts of many cities during the Second World War.
Contents page: Women workers played an essential part in the industrial boom of wartime USA.

First published in 1994 by
Wayland (Publishers) Ltd
61 Western Rd, Hove
East Sussex BN3 1JD, England

© Copyright 1994 Wayland (Publishers) Ltd

Book editor: Katrina Maitland Smith
Series editor: Paul Mason
Designer: Mark Whitchurch

British Library Cataloguing in Publication Data
   Cross, Robin
   Cities at War-(Era of the Second World
   War Series)
   I.Title II.Series
   940.53

ISBN 0-7502-1224-1

Typeset in the UK by Mark Whitchurch
Printed and bound in Italy by
Rotolito Lombarda S.p.A.

Picture acknowledgements
The publishers gratefully acknowledge the permission of the following to use their photographs in this book: Archiv für Kunst und Geschichte, Berlin/Image Select cover,14, 20, 35, 38, 40; Camera Press 23, 24, 37; Mary Evans/Alexander Meledin Collection 43; The Hulton-Deutsch Collection 4 (bottom), 6, 7, 9, 10, 16, 19, 22, 25, 26, 27, 31, 36; Peter Newark's Historical Pictures 18; Peter Newark's Military Pictures 39 (bottom), 41, 42; PHOTRI 11, 12-13; Popperfoto 34; Topham Picture Source 4 (top), 8, 17, 21(bottom), 28, 33, 39 (top); Warner Bros./Joel Finler Collection 15; Wayland Picture Library 30, 32.
Artwork by John Yates 5, 21(top), 29, 44.

Contents

Introduction

This book sets out to examine the differing experiences of seven cities during the Second World War. Their fortunes varied. When peace came in 1945, Leningrad lay in ruins. In contrast, Los Angeles was entering a period of great material prosperity.

Some wartime experiences were shared. Bombs fell on five of the seven cities in this study. The black-out, rationing and the increased role in war work played by women were factors common to most of them. But even here the experience was very different from city to city. In London, as in the rest of Britain, food

In the ruins of postwar Japan, a citizen of Tokyo takes a drink from a shattered water main.

A church in Berlin goes up in flames during a heavy Allied air raid.

rationing led to an improved diet for its citizens, particularly the poorest. In Warsaw the reality of rationing was much grimmer, leaving many on the edge of starvation. In Tokyo at the end of the war people survived by eating weeds.

The main emphasis here, however, is on the aspects of each city's wartime history which made special and lasting marks on its landscape and the lives of its citizens. The Blitz in London remains the central image of the English capital's ability to endure under fire. The siege of Leningrad witnessed one of the most dramatic examples of the terrible sacrifices made by the Russian people during the war. In Warsaw, German occupation meant terror and persecution for the Polish, and in Berlin, during the final days of the War, the Third Reich fell amid a sea of suffering and destruction.

The result is a panorama of the impact of war on seven of the great cities of the world.

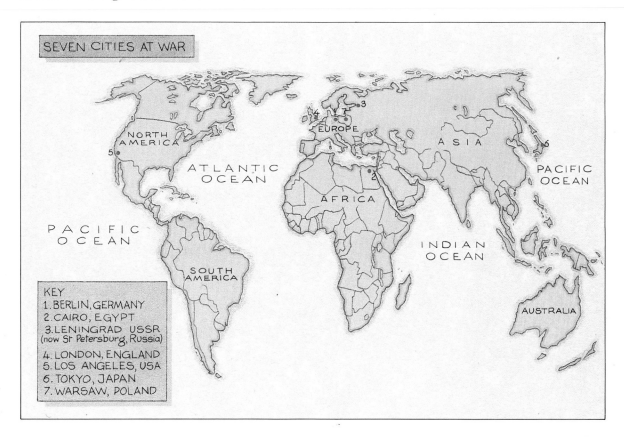

SEVEN CITIES AT WAR

KEY
1. BERLIN, GERMANY
2. CAIRO, EGYPT
3. LENINGRAD USSR
(now St Petersburg, Russia)
4. LONDON, ENGLAND
5. LOS ANGELES, USA
6. TOKYO, JAPAN
7. WARSAW, POLAND

Tokyo

On the eve of the Second World War, which began on 3 September 1939, Japan had already been at war with China for two years and was looking towards a wider empire in the Far East. Japan was the most industrialized nation in Asia. Fifty per cent of its population of 73 million were crammed into its great manufacturing cities - Osaka, Nagoya, Kyōto, Kōbe, Yokohama and the Japanese capital, Tokyo.

The conflict in Europe was nearly two and a half years old when Japan entered the war after launching a surprise attack on the US naval base at Pearl Harbor. The aim was to disable US naval air power in order to give Japan freedom of movement. In the following six months of the war in the Far East the Japanese cut a swathe through the Pacific, gaining vast territories for their Greater East Asia Co-Prosperity Sphere.

But Japan had awakened a sleeping military giant, the United States of America, whose industrial strength was greater than that of Japan and its German ally combined. Against such a powerful enemy defeat was inevitable.

An aerial view of the centre of Tokyo taken in December 1941, the month that Japan went to war in the Far East.

Japan's position was made particularly difficult by the fact that its people depended on imported food to survive and its war factories depended on imported raw materials to maintain production. The ships which carried the rice, rubber, coal, iron ore and, above all, oil back to Japan were sunk in increasingly large numbers by US submarines. As the war continued, the Japanese war economy was slowly strangled to death. By the end of the war all of Japan's merchant ships had been sent to the bottom of the sea by US torpedoes.

People from a poor district in Tokyo queue for food. The people of Japan depended on imported food, and as the US Navy sank more and more of Japan's merchant ships food became scarcer and scarcer.

Food shortages worsened and war production suffered further because people were spending so much time waiting in ration queues or scouring the countryside for scarce food supplies. Children suffered too. When Japanese boys and girls were measured in 1946, the year after the war ended, they were found on average to be 3cm shorter than their counterparts of 1937. During the war, many Japanese children suffered from rickets, a bone disease caused by a lack of calcium, because supplies of milk (a major source of calcium) were so scarce.

Throughout the war, the Japanese were bombarded with more propaganda than the people of any other fighting nation. Those who showed the slightest sign of questioning the government line ran the risk of being interrogated and imprisoned by an agency with the sinister name of the Thought Police.

War shortages

By 1943 the citizens of Tokyo were beginning to feel the pinch. New clothes were made from a flimsy cloth consisting of tiny amounts of cotton woven with wood pulp and tree bark. Leather supplies were commandeered by the army, bringing an end to the manufacture of new shoes for civilians. The Japanese took to wearing wooden clogs, dubbed 'patriotic footwear'.

Pre-war shoes were saved for special occasions. In November 1944, a winter clothing distribution in Tokyo provided the equivalent of one pair of socks for every fourth person and one towel for every 15 people. Civilian motor cars disappeared from the streets. People rode bicycles to work until the rubber tyres wore out. Then they walked.

Students build air-raid shelters in the streets of Tokyo. The shelters provided little protection against the massive American air raids which began in March 1945.

At a local level, people's lives were dominated by neighbourhood associations, the *Tonarigumi*, each of which contained about a dozen households. These associations handled everything from food rationing to making civil defence preparations against US bombing raids. The members of the *Tonarigumi* learned to identify enemy planes and how to deal with incendiary bombs. They conducted fire drills and dug trenches in local parks to serve as public air-raid shelters. They patrolled the streets to enforce the black-out and made sure that each family kept a rucksack of rice and medicine for emergencies. They also helped to demolish thousands of buildings to create stretches of open ground, called fire-breaks, which would prevent fire from racing through the city.

These activities increased the sense of common purpose but also led to a false sense of security. In reality, Tokyo, like all of Japan's cities, was a huge tinder-box. The concrete office buildings in its centre were surrounded by a sea of wood and paper houses, most of them jammed together only a few inches apart. There were few big public air-raid shelters. The 'foxholes' people dug for their families in their back gardens rapidly filled with water. The government quarried tunnels into the hills outside Tokyo, but these were too far away to provide immediate shelter during an air raid.

For some time the islands of Japan remained beyond the range of land-based US bombers. But the capture of the Mariana Islands in the summer of 1944 gave the USA a springboard 2,500km from Tokyo from which to launch its B-29 heavy bombers.

The match was put to the Tokyo tinder-box on the night of 9/10 March 1945 when nearly 300 B-29s launched a devastating incendiary raid on Tokyo. Fire-breaks, 'foxholes' and buckets filled with sand were useless against the fires which broke out in the densely populated working-class Koto district, where most of the bombs fell. A cold 65kmh wind spread the fires rapidly.

Eastern Tokyo was wiped off the map. Overnight the US bombers destroyed 20 per cent of the city's war industry and about 60 per cent of its business district. Over 250,000 buildings were burned down, driving at least one million survivors to the countryside. It took the authorities over three weeks to clear the streets of the charred bodies of those who had died in the fires. The death toll was at least 100,000.

One witness to the incendiary raid was journalist Matsuo Kato. He saw hundreds of small fires whipped into *'great walls of flame, which began leaping streets, fire-breaks and canals at dazzling speed.'*[1] The flames overtook those running to safety. Those who were not burned to death were suffocated as the fires sucked the oxygen out of the air. They died, *'like so many fish left gasping on the bottom of a lake that has been drained.'*[1a] Thousands of people tried to escape the flames by jumping into the Sumida River and the city's network of canals. Many drowned in the crush or were boiled to death as the water was heated by the fires. The next day rescue units retrieved the bodies. The head of one such unit, Dr Kubota Shigenori, recalled: *'In the black Sumida river countless bodies were floating, clothed bodies, naked bodies, all black as charcoal... These were dead people but you couldn't tell whether they were men or women. You couldn't even tell if the objects floating by were arms and legs or pieces of burnt wood.'*[2]

The flattened industrial district of Tokyo photographed in the late summer of 1945. Only a few steel-structured buildings still stand amid a sea of rubble.

More fire raids followed. On 25 May, 500 B-29s dropped 4,000 tonnes of bombs on the residential sections in northern and western Tokyo. There was little or no looting after these raids. In any case, there was almost nothing left to be stolen. The *Tonarigumi* did their best to maintain order and an appearance of normality amid the destruction. Many people clung to superstitions, believing that eating pickled plums or red beans with rice would protect them from the bombs.

Such food was almost unobtainable. The citizens of Tokyo survived by eating thistles, mugwort and chickweed. They gathered acorns and ground them into flour. Stray cats and dogs were killed and eaten.

Japan surrendered on 15 August 1945, after the USA had dropped atomic bombs on the cities of Hiroshima and Nagasaki. The head of a Tokyo *Tonarigumi*, Suto Ryosaku, listened to the Japanese Emperor Hirohito announce the end of the war in a radio broadcast. For most Japanese it was the first time they had heard the Emperor's voice: *'All of us sank into silence... I felt in a daze, exasperated, and tears of resentment began to flow... The woman on duty for the* Tonarigumi *came, so I asked her what she thought about the end of the war. She was surprisingly calm and bright-eyed – perhaps because the fear of the raids had disappeared and the bitter work of preventing fires had ended. Although most people think that defeat is extremely depressing, in their hearts they seem generally relieved.'* [3]

A Japanese boy surveys the wreckage of his school.

Los Angeles

On 7 December 1941, Japan launched a surprise attack on the great US naval base at Pearl Harbor on the Hawaiian island of Oahu. The next day, the USA declared war on Japan.

J. Edgar Hoover, chief of the Federal Bureau of Investigation (FBI) at the time, ordered the rounding-up of Japanese nationals living on the West Coast of America. At the baseball ground in Hollywood, the world's movie capital, the Paramount studio team was playing a team of Japanese nationals living in California. The FBI men let the game finish – Paramount won – before arresting the Japanese.

In California a bigger round-up followed. In February 1942 President Franklin D. Roosevelt signed an order which led to the internment of 120,000 people of Japanese descent, two-thirds of them US citizens. The Japanese-Americans were interned in a number of bleak camps in remote parts of America's Western states.

The people of Los Angeles feared a Japanese air attack. In February 1942 there occurred the so-called Battle of Los Angeles in which American fighter aircraft, alerted by mistaken radar information, chased each other round the sky in search of a non-existent enemy.

Fear of invasion

Throughout the USA the reaction to the attack on Pearl Harbor was one of disbelief followed by anger. On the Pacific coast there was an added element of panic.
A radio station announced that a Japanese invasion was on the way. Thousands of men armed with rifles and pistols rushed to the City Hall in Los Angeles, ready to repel the imaginary invaders.

Japanese-Americans on their way to an internment camp in 1942.

The Japanese never came. Unlike the other principal combatants in the Second World War, the United States was not bombed or invaded by the enemy. When the war ended in 1945, large tracts of Europe and the Far East lay in ruins. In contrast, the United States and its people had entered an era of unparalleled prosperity. The demands of war had produced a huge industrial surge in America. By 1945 the economic power of the United States was almost equal to that of the rest of the world combined. Industrial output had nearly doubled, as had the weekly earnings of the average factory worker. Farmers' incomes had increased fourfold.

Nowhere was this explosion of economic activity more evident than in California. The US government poured some $70 billion of investment into California during the war. California made good use of the money. Its large urban centres contained thousands of small machine shops, auto assembly and food preserving plants, and clothing manufacturers which could convert to wartime production at the drop of a hat. Its big shipyards and aircraft plants had survived the worst effects of the economic slump of the 1930s. Its position on the Pacific coast was ideal for waging war against Japan.

Industrial prosperity

During the war the value of California's industrial output rose from $2.7 billion in 1939 to $10.1 billion in 1944. Los Angeles accounted for half of California's war production, with aircraft and shipbuilding taking the lion's share. By 1939 the Los Angeles area was well-established as the main aircraft manufacturing centre in the **USA**. Of the 350,000 aircraft workers employed on the Pacific coast more than two-thirds worked in southern California at factories owned by Douglas, Lockheed, North American Aviation, Northrop and Hughes Aircraft. In 1940, the United States was producing only about 2,000 aircraft a year. Four years later, with the end of the war in sight, annual output had risen to nearly 100,000.

Shipbuilding and the associated steel industry also played a vital part in the wartime economy of Los Angeles. At Terminal Island were the vast yards of the Californian Shipbuilding Company. To supply them with the prefabricated steel they needed, the Fortuna steel mills were built nearby.

These great industries were supported by hundreds of smaller plants in the area producing everything from machine tools to synthetic rubber. Even more jobs were generated by large military installations like the **US Naval** dry docks, also at Terminal Island. As a result the war years saw a rise in employment in the Los Angeles area, and in southern California generally, which was as much as four times the national average.

War work: women on the production line in the Douglas Aircraft plant at Long Beach, California. These all-women crews are putting the finishing touches to the nose sections of American bomber aircraft.

The industrial boom created millions of new jobs which drew people to California from all parts of the USA. One of the features of American society has been its mobility – the readiness of people to tear up their roots and travel long distances to start a new life. The breakneck industrial expansion in wartime California, which has been compared to a modern-day Gold Rush, increased the population of Los Angeles by at least half a million people. With increased population went growing productivity. By the end of the war, factories across the whole of the Los Angeles area were turning out 10 per cent of the total US war output.

Economic success was accompanied by social problems. The fast pace of life in the urban sprawl of wartime Los Angeles, and the frequently long journeys between home and work, led to a high rate of absenteeism in war factories. In the first six weeks of 1943 one aircraft plant took on 150,000 workers, and 138,000 workers left. Many people who had come to California from the rural Midwest were unable to cope with the long-distance commuting – usually by car – across the city. In the Los Angeles area women made up nearly half the workforce in aircraft plants. Holding down a full-time job and caring for a family often proved too much for them, in spite of the assistance of a child-care programme sponsored by the government.

Disruption to family life

There was another dark side to the wartime economic miracle. There was racial tension between whites and the blacks and Mexicans who had come to California in search of work in the war plants. Violent crime increased. The police reported a steep rise in juvenile delinquency. They blamed it on the disruption that the war had brought to family life, with fathers away at the war and mothers working in war factories. The police attempted to impose a 9pm curfew on youths under the age of 17, but there were too few police officers to enforce the measure.

Right: A female factory worker takes the strain in 1943. Women workers played a vital part in war production.

Hollywood goes to war

From the 1920s Los Angeles' most famous export had been the movies. Hollywood, a suburb of the city, was the world's greatest dream factory, a byword for luxury and glamour.

The war had cut the Hollywood studios off from many of their overseas markets. But there was a huge increase in cinema audiences at home. With industry prospering, war workers had money to spend and wanted escapist entertainment.

The US government also realized the importance of film as propaganda, and the studios quickly converted to the demands of war. The familiar categories of film – crime thrillers, musicals and Westerns – could be made to include popular war themes.

Patriotism proved immensely profitable for big studios like MGM, Paramount and Warner Bros. In 1943 the number of films dealing either directly or indirectly with the war reached a peak. As the war drew to a close there was a greater demand for pure escapism in the form of frothy musicals or exciting costume adventures.

The stars threw themselves into the war effort, promoting War Bond drives, touring the battle fronts or entertaining servicemen on leave at the famous Hollywood Canteen. There a lucky GI might be served a hamburger by a glamorous leading lady such as Joan Crawford, or be treated to a dance by the forces' favourite pin-up girl, Betty Grable.

Released in 1943, Warner Bros.' Casablanca remains one of the classic wartime movies.

The arrival of so many newcomers in Los Angeles produced a housing shortage. To cut down the commuting problems, new housing units were built near the war plants they served. Los Angeles was the automobile capital of the world, where a car was as much a necessity as a luxury. Over 85 per cent of the workers in Los Angeles travelled to work by car, causing a major air pollution problem. By 1945 the notorious Los Angeles smog was so thick on some days that it was considered a danger to military air traffic.

Southern California emerged from the war as one of the powerhouses of the US economy. Its war factories were at the leading edge of military high-technology, particularly in aviation. The war years laid the foundations of the great California-based military-industrial corporations that were to play a dominant part in US economic life in the post-war years.

London

It was 11.15am on the sunny Sunday morning of 3 September 1939. In London, and across Britain, families gathered round their radios to hear the Prime Minister, Neville Chamberlain, announce that Britain was at war with Germany.

Within minutes, the eerie wail of air-raid sirens sounded over London. The warning was a false alarm. The incoming aircraft was a lone French civilian plane. This established the mood of the next seven months: an uneasy lull dubbed the Phoney War which came to an end when Germany invaded France and the Low Countries of The Netherlands, Belgium and Luxembourg in the spring of 1940.

No bombs had fallen on London, but everywhere were the sights and sounds of war. About 1.5 million children were evacuated from London. Everyone was issued with uncomfortable gas masks because it was assumed that the Germans would drop poison gas on the British capital. In thousands of back gardens, Londoners erected Anderson shelters, simple refuges from bombs which were to save many lives. Piles of sandbags appeared around public and private buildings to protect against bomb blast. Windows were secured with criss-cross swathes of tape to stop them shattering. Billowing barrage balloons flew overhead to ward off low-flying enemy aircraft.

London women grapple with parts of an Anderson Shelter in 1939. The shelter provided protection from everything except a direct hit.

Men of London's Auxiliary Fire Service fight the flames. On the worst nights, London's fire service had to deal with up to 2,000 separate fires across the city.

For every dockside warehouse there seemed to be a different kind of fire. There were pepper fires, filling firemen's lungs with stinging particles; rum fires spilling rivers of flaming liquid into the streets; and rubber fires producing dense clouds of suffocating smoke. Blazing barges, cut loose from their moorings, drifted down the River Thames, adding to the chaos.

The German bombers finally came on 7 September 1940. Three hundred aircraft dropped over 300 tonnes of high-explosives and thousands of incendiary bombs on London's docks, and the closely packed streets of the East End. Entire streets of flimsy terraced houses were reduced to dust and rubble. In the docks, blazing warehouses lit the way for 250 more bombers which, between 8pm and dawn, dropped another 300 tonnes of bombs. To a fire officer battling the blaze in the Surrey docks it seemed that *'the whole world was on fire.'*

For the next 56 nights, London was bombed from dusk to dawn. The bombers followed the silver line of the Thames to strike at the biggest target in the world. Londoners quickly coined a nickname for the nightly bombing; they called it the Blitz.

Immediately after the first air raids in September, the authorities in London had to face a problem they had not anticipated. Before the war, government planners had expected that a heavy air attack on London would kill hundreds of thousands of people within weeks, and that tens of thousands more would be driven mad by the bombing. In the first two nights of the Blitz nearly 1,000 people were killed, a depressing figure but a fraction of what the government had feared. Dealing with the dead proved easier than coping with the thousands who remained alive but homeless.

By the end of 1940 the death toll from bombing in London had reached 13,600, with many thousands more injured. But over 250,000 Londoners had been made homeless. The morale of London's citizens had been badly shaken in the first two weeks of the Blitz, when the city's emergency services could not deal with the task of rehousing and feeding thousands of homeless. Many of them were left with little but the dirt-caked clothes in which they had emerged from the ruins of their homes. But as the weeks passed many people were amazed to discover that life was bearable in spite of the bombs.

Amid the ruins of their street, an East End family sits down to a meal with bombed-out neighbours during the Blitz.

The people of London kept up their daily routines in the middle of the strange new sensations of the Blitz: the warning wail of the sirens; the menacing throb of the approaching bombers; the sound of high-explosive bombs falling, which was likened to a huge sheet being torn in the sky; streets bathed in the ghostly blue-and-white glare of incendiary bombs; and the distinctive smell of bombed-out buildings, a mixture of dust, smoke, charred wood and escaping gas.

London carries on. A milkman picks his way through the rubble to make a doorstep delivery in October 1940.

This new way of life revolved around the nightly routine of being bombed. A survey conducted in November 1940 revealed the surprising fact that only about 40 per cent of Londoners took shelter from the bombs – the rest preferred to take their chance in bed or under the stairs. Of those who did take shelter, only about nine in every hundred used public shelters. Another four in every hundred took refuge in the stations of London's Underground system. By late September the London Tube was playing host to about 180,000 people every night. Many had queued all day to secure their place underground. When the trains stopped running for the night, the current was cut off in the electric rails and the shelterers settled down to sleep on the platforms, in the passageways, on the escalators and even between the rails.

Not all the Tube stations proved safe. On the night of 14 October 1940 a direct hit burst a water main running over the station in Balham High Street, burying 64 people under a torrent of mud and sludge.

The final phase of the Blitz began on 16 April 1941, when nearly 700 bombers raided London. It ended on the night of 10 May, when an attack by 500 bombers started over 2,000 separate fires across London. The next day, one-third of the city's streets were impassable. Even those whose houses had survived the bombing were often left without gas, electricity or water.

Squalor in Stepney

One of the most notorious shelters used by the public was a huge underground goods yard under the Tilbury railway arches. Every night as many as 16,000 people sheltered there. Conditions were foul, as one observer recalled: 'The first time I went in there, I had to come out, I felt sick. You couldn't see anything, you could just smell the fug, the overwhelming stench... There were thousands and thousands of people lying head to toe, all along the bays and with no facilities. At the beginning there were only four earth buckets down the far end behind screens for toilets. It was terribly hard on the old people because they were obviously terrified. They'd usually come down in their pyjamas and dressing-gowns and they'd have to sit up all night huddled together. The place was a hell hole.'[5]

In London since September 1940 some 220,000 houses had been destroyed and another 1.5 million made uninhabitable. In the worst-hit areas in the East End four out of every ten houses had been wrecked. In eight months of bombing just over 20,000 Londoners had lost their lives.

By the end of June 1941, two-thirds of the German air force had been withdrawn from the campaign against Britain and transferred to support Adolf Hitler's invasion of the USSR. Heavy raids on London were replaced by attacks on the ports along Britain's southern coast. In the capital the big clean-up was underway. Over 16,000 building repairers were at work. By the early summer they had made over a million damaged homes wind and weatherproof. In the end, the sheer size of the city had proved too much for the German air force.

A rescue squad pulls a survivor from a bombed house in November 1940.

Warsaw

THE BREAK-UP OF POLAND IN 1939

0 miles 100
0 Km 160

EAST PRUSSIA

USSR

GERMANY

• Warsaw

P O L A N D

CZECHOSLOVAKIA

• Cracow

AUSTRIA

ROMANIA

Poland before German and Soviet Invasions

☐ Occupied by Germany 1939

▨ Occupied by USSR 1939

1939 Border of General Government

Border of General Government after German invasion of USSR

The Second World War became inevitable on 1 September 1939 when Germany invaded Poland. The Germans achieved a swift victory, and on 27 September they entered Warsaw, the Polish capital. Defeated Poland was then divided between Germany and the USSR, which had invaded Poland from the east on 17 September. It was the beginning of a long nightmare for the people of Poland.

The German aim was not to dominate Poland but to destroy it as a separate nation. Most of German-occupied Poland was made part of the German empire. The remainder, including Warsaw, became the General Government of Occupied Poland. In the summer of 1941, when Germany invaded the USSR, the Germans took over the Polish territory occupied by the Soviets since September 1939.

Warsaw ceased to be the capital of Poland; its role was taken over by Cracow in southern Poland. This became the base of the General Government headed by a ruthless German lawyer, Dr Hans Frank. The Germans began to turn Warsaw into a German city. Public buildings were draped with flags displaying the Nazi symbol of the swastika. German street names replaced Polish ones. Many buildings damaged in the fighting of September 1939 were deliberately left unrepaired by the Germans to remind the Poles of their humiliating defeat. Polish-language newspapers were banned. Poles of German

Below: Dr Hans Frank, Nazi Governor-General of Poland. He was executed for war crimes in 1946.

Efforts to survive

Life for the Poles in Warsaw became a matter of day-to-day survival. The Germans controlled the food supply. They lived off the fat of the land while the Poles starved. Polish ration allowances provided for only a quarter of the daily calorie intake needed by a healthy adult. This reduced resistance to disease. The death rate rose sharply, pushed up by lack of fuel for the winter, overcrowded housing, and a shortage of soap, clean linen, drugs and decent medical facilities. To survive, the Poles had to help each other. Vegetable gardens sprang up on every vacant piece of land in Warsaw, even on the strips of grass that ran down the city's broad avenues. Charities fed and clothed the needy. In 1941 at least one quarter of Warsaw's inhabitants depended on public relief measures. Those who could afford it bought scarce items in the flourishing black market.

descent were forced to accept German nationality. Those who refused risked the death penalty.

The Nazis had decided that the Poles were to become their slaves. Polish leaders were executed or sent to concentration camps. Polish universities, secondary schools and libraries were closed down. The teaching of Polish history was forbidden. No Pole was to be allowed to rise higher than the level of factory foreman. The rest were to form a huge pool of cheap labour for the Germans.

The Germans enforced these measures with a policy of terror. Street round-ups and mass public executions were commonplace. In Warsaw between October 1943 and February 1944 daily executions were claiming the lives of up to 300 people a week.

During the war, the greatest physical change to Warsaw was made by the Warsaw Ghetto. Nazi racial persecution led to the creation of a closed quarter of the city in which the Jews of Warsaw were confined. On 15 November 1940 the Ghetto was sealed off from the rest of the city by a 3m high wall which stretched for 18km. Access to the outside world was by 22 gates guarded by German and Polish police. Jews could be executed for travelling to other parts of Warsaw without proper authorization. Contact with the Germans was maintained by the *Judenrat*, the

German troops round up Jews in the Warsaw Ghetto in 1943. The Jews were transported to death camps where they were murdered.

24-member Jewish Council, which kept order with its own police force and organized the forced labour battalions that were demanded by the Germans.

Packed inside the Ghetto were 430,000 people, the original population swelled by refugees from other Jewish communities in Poland. The result was starvation and disease. Typhus raged in the Ghetto. In the summer of 1941 it was killing 5,000 people a month. In December 1941 it was estimated that over 200,000 people in the Ghetto were without food or shelter. Many had to sell their clothes, their only possessions, and wear rags. Small children lived and died on the streets. Corpses lay in the open, covered with sheets of newspaper.

Small Jewish boys scurry through a hole in the wall surrounding the Warsaw Ghetto. Jews who ventured outside the Ghetto ran the risk of execution if they were caught.

On 22 July 1942 the Germans began the systematic murder of all the Jews in the Ghetto. Over the next two months about 265,000 men, women and children were deported to the death camp at Treblinka, 80km west of Warsaw, where they were killed.

In the Ghetto

Before she escaped from the Warsaw Ghetto 16-year-old Janina Bauman kept a diary, noting all that she saw. On 18 April 1941, she wrote: 'Two little boys are begging in the street next to our gate. I see them every time I go out... Their heads are shaven, clothes in rags, their frightfully emaciated, tiny faces bring to mind birds rather than human beings. Their huge black eyes, though, are human; so full of sadness... The younger one may be five or six, the older ten, perhaps. They don't move, they don't speak. The little one just sits on the pavement, the bigger one just stands there with his claw of a hand stretched out. I must remember now to bring them some food whenever I go out.'[6]

Latvian troops fighting alongside the Germans view their grim handiwork – the slaughter of defenceless Jewish men and women in a doorway in the Warsaw Ghetto.

After these deportations young Jews in the Ghetto organized themselves into the Jewish Fighting Organization and made plans for armed resistance to the Germans. On 19 April 1943 German troops were sent into the Ghetto with orders to clear out its remaining inhabitants and destroy the buildings. Warsaw was to be 'Jew-free' by Adolf Hitler's birthday, the following day.

The Germans met with fierce resistance from about 1,000 Jewish fighters armed with rifles, pistols and home-made bombs. For a month the Jews fought a desperate battle against overwhelming odds. The Germans used aircraft, tanks and flame-throwers against them, reducing the Ghetto to smouldering rubble.

On 10 May SS troops blew up the Ghetto's Jerusalem synagogue. Their commander, General Jurgen Stroop, declared *'the Jewish quarter of Warsaw is no more.'* But fighting continued for several days before the Germans were able to complete the destruction of the Ghetto.

Resistance to the Nazis
The Jews knew that resistance could end only in defeat. But they were determined to strike back at their tormentors rather than submit quietly to death in the gas chambers. Theirs had been the first popular uprising against the Nazis anywhere in occupied Europe, an heroic gesture that inspired other enemies of Nazism.

Only a handful of Jews – possibly as few as 100 – survived the uprising and escaped to the Polish side of the city. The remainder, some 60,000 people, either died in the fighting or were captured and sent to the death camps. German casualties are unknown: estimates vary between 100 and 700 killed.

The Germans had not crushed the spirit of the Poles. From the earliest days of the German occupation, the Poles had organized an underground resistance movement. In Warsaw it published over 100 secret newspapers while its members armed themselves to attack the Germans. The armed wing of the underground was the Polish Home Army. The men and women of the Home Army were loyal to the exiled Polish government which had retreated to London. However, in the summer of 1944 there was another Polish government-in-waiting. The Soviets were driving the Germans out of Poland. In July they liberated the city of Lublin in eastern Poland, and set up the Lublin Committee, a body of Polish Communists who were to be placed in power and controlled by the USSR when Poland was liberated.

In Warsaw, the Home Army had been gathering its strength, waiting for the moment when the Germans were weak enough for the Poles to strike a blow for their independence. For some time, the Soviet radio stations had been making Polish-language broadcasts calling for an uprising against the Germans. Now the Red Army was only 19km from Warsaw.

The desolate scene left by the destruction of the Warsaw Ghetto by the Germans in May 1943. About 6,000 Jews were left buried under the rubble.

On the morning of 1 August, with the approval of the Polish government-in-exile in London, the Home Army in Warsaw went on to the attack under the command of General Tadeusz Bor Komorowski. The Germans were taken by surprise. Within four days the Home Army and its civilian helpers had gained control of about three-fifths of Warsaw. But the Soviets did not come to help. They remained in their positions to the south and east of Warsaw as the battle raged inside the city.

Polish volunteers drag off a dead horse to roast during the Warsaw uprising in 1944. Starving and with few weapons, the Poles managed to hold out for two months against overwhelming odds.

The Germans recovered and fed reinforcements into the city. The Poles were gradually pushed back into ever-shrinking pockets of resistance. In Warsaw's Old City, whose 100,000 inhabitants huddled in their cellars, the Home Army's district commander wrote in his diary on 29 August: *'No food, little water, bad sanitary conditions, little sign of speedy help.'*

In Warsaw, the resistance continued for two months. Children joined the fight. Young girls carrying messages crawled for miles through the city's sewers to avoid snipers' bullets.

The Soviets wait

Still the Soviets stayed put. The Red Army was exhausted and short of supplies, but there were other reasons for denying help to the Poles. The Home Army was a potential opponent of the Polish Communist Party, and Joseph Stalin, the Communist Soviet leader, wanted it out of the way. He decided to let the Germans do the work for him.

The British begged the Soviets to allow their aircraft to fly over Warsaw, drop supplies to the Poles and then fly on to land in Soviet territory. The request was refused. Some supplies were eventually flown in from Italy, but most of what was dropped fell into German hands as the Polish-held areas grew smaller and smaller.

As the Poles were pushed back street by street the Germans took terrible revenge. Captured Polish fighters were shot on the spot, as were the doctors and nurses tending the wounded. Their bodies were piled up, drenched with petrol and then set alight. Polish civilians were marched in front of German tanks as human shields.

On 10 September the Soviets finally advanced on Warsaw, but they failed to break through to the city. On 2 October Bor Komorowski, the Polish general, surrendered to the Germans. In the uprising at least 200,000 Polish civilians and 15,000 members of the Polish Home Army had died. They had inflicted 20,000 casualties on the Germans, of whom 10,000 had been killed. The Germans granted the captured Polish fighters the status of prisoners of war. Over 15,000 of them, including 2,000 women and children, were marched off to prison camps. Behind them they left a city in ruins.

The Germans were not driven out of Warsaw until January 1945. Though German occupation was exchanged for Soviet domination, Warsaw became the capital of Poland once more, and the city was rebuilt by its people.

German troops advance through the ruins of Warsaw's Old Town as the uprising nears its end. The Germans put down the uprising with great brutality, using execution squads made up of released convicts.

Cairo

Pre-war tourists in Cairo put on special shoes to enter the city's Muhammad Ali mosque.

In the autumn of 1940 Cairo, the capital of Egypt, seemed a world away from Britain. In Britain, the immediate threat of a German cross-Channel invasion was receding, but it was replaced by the nightly bombardment of London by the Luftwaffe. Soon the Blitz, as it became known, would also strike at Britain's major ports and industrial cities. At this point in the war a British civilian living in the East End of London stood a far higher chance of being killed by enemy action than a British soldier stationed in Egypt.

In Britain, rationing had been in force for nine months. In Cairo, the corner shops and food stores were crammed with the fresh fruit, butter, eggs and coffee that were fast becoming a distant memory in Britain. The city's famous Shepheard's Hotel did not run out of champagne until 1943. In Cairo's fashionable department stores it was business as usual. Shelves groaned under the weight of luxury goods. There was no rationing here.

Egypt was nominally an independent country, but it was also a vital piece in the centre of the British empire. From 1882 the British had controlled Egypt through military occupation. Control of Egypt meant control of the Suez Canal, which connected the Mediterranean and Red Seas. For the British, the Suez Canal was the vital link with India, the richest part of the empire.

In 1936 the Anglo-Egyptian Treaty transformed the occupation into a military alliance between the two countries. The Egyptians gained greater independence from Britain, but British troops remained on Egyptian soil. The only embassy in Cairo was the British embassy.

When war broke out in 1939, Egypt broke off diplomatic relations with Germany but did not declare war. After Italy entered the war on the side of Germany in June 1940 the British used Egypt as the base for their military operations in North Africa and the Middle East. Cairo became the British General Headquarters (GHQ) Middle East.

Egyptian support for the British was less than wholehearted as the desert war flowed back and forth in North Africa. Many Egyptian nationalists wanted an Axis victory to free them of the British. A secret anti-British organization was formed within the Egyptian armed forces. Among its members were two future Presidents of Egypt, Gamal Abdel Nasser and Anwar Sadat.

Egyptians and Europeans

There was much anti-British feeling in Egypt. It was particularly strong among students and young officers in the Egyptian army. They wanted to rid Egypt of all European influence. But the prosperous Egyptian middle class copied the Western dress and manners of the Europeans living there. British, French, Italian and Greek traders, technicians and administrators ran the greater part of the Egyptian economy. A great gulf separated the Europeans from the mass of ordinary Egyptians in Cairo, who lived in the teeming slums which surrounded the city, sweltering in the summer and shivering in the winter. Their lives scarcely touched each other at all.

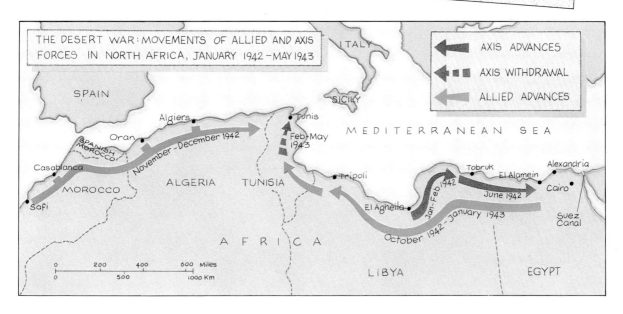

The war in North Africa flowed back and forth over a relatively thin coastal strip. To the south much of the desert was impassable. Both sides fought to capture the supply ports on the coast.

The Desert Fox: German General Erwin Rommel (1891-1944), commander of the Afrika Korps. A master of mobile operations, Rommel was eventually halted and defeated at the Second Battle of El Alamein in November 1942.

The young King of Egypt, Farouk, who had succeeded to the throne in 1936, could not be relied upon by the British. He refused to dismiss the Italian servants who surrounded him. He had the power to make things very awkward for the British by appointing ministers who were openly hostile to them. As early as 1940, the British ambassador in Cairo, Sir Miles Lampson, suggested that the British government force Farouk to abdicate.

The Anglo-Egyptian Treaty had guaranteed Egypt's right to run her own internal affairs. The British, however, did not hesitate to tear it up when the desert war boiled up into a crisis in January 1942. The German General, Erwin Rommel, commander of the Afrika Korps, had gone on to the offensive and regained most of the territory he had lost to the British in the fighting of November-December 1941. For the British, the stability of Egypt had never been more vital. On 4 February they surrounded Farouk's Abdin Palace in Cairo with troops and armoured cars. Inside the palace Sir Miles Lampson told Farouk that he was 'not fit to rule'. Farouk did not abdicate but agreed to the appointment of a new Prime Minister, Nahas Pasha. The British had decided that only Nahas Pasha and his party, the Wafd, had sufficient strength to maintain a government in Egypt in difficult wartime conditions. However, there were few Egyptians prepared to forgive or forget the humiliation of their King by the British.

By the summer of 1942, there were over 140,000 Allied troops based in Cairo, housed in hot and dusty camps strung around the city. The British no longer feared a nationalist uprising by the Egyptians. But when Rommel advanced into Egypt in June 1942 it was clear that he would be welcomed by many Egyptians. The Afrika Korps was only 100km from the Egyptian port of Alexandria on the Mediterranean coast. Egyptian shopkeepers in Alexandria and Cairo made sure that they had photographs of Rommel and Adolf Hitler to slip into a frame when the Germans arrived.

Cairo was seized by a panic which became known as The Flap. Rumours raced through the city that the Germans would take over within 24 hours. At the British embassy and GHQ the staff made bonfires of vast quantities of secret files. On what was dubbed Ash Wednesday, charred flakes of paper floated over Cairo like black snow. The railway station was jammed with women and children waiting to be evacuated to South Africa and Palestine. Sir Miles Lampson displayed his coolness in the middle of crisis by ordering the embassy railings to be repainted, making the point that he, at least, expected to remain in Cairo for some time. Meanwhile, Anwar Sadat was preparing a treaty to present to Rommel, promising to raise an army to fight against the British in return for complete independence.

British troops dig trenches in the shadow of the Pyramids on the outskirts of Cairo in the opening months of the war.

Allied troops in Cairo
There was a dramatic contrast between the luxuries of life in Cairo - with its restaurants, nightclubs and moonlight trips to the Pyramids - and the harsh conditions of desert warfare. Fighting troops referred to those stationed permanently in Cairo as 'Groppi's Light Horse', after the city's two famous bars named Groppi's.

Men of the British Eighth Army advance during the Second Battle of El Alamein in which Rommel was defeated.

Rommel never reached Cairo. At the beginning of July 1942 his advance was checked at the First Battle of El Alamein. Four months later he was decisively defeated by General Montgomery at the Second Battle of El Alamein. On 4 November, Rommel began to retreat westward across the desert. The Flap was over.

As the war moved away from Cairo, the city briefly became a centre of international politics. In November 1943, the British Prime Minister Winston Churchill met the US President Franklin D. Roosevelt and the Chinese Nationalist leader Chiang Kai-Shek in Cairo. At the Cairo conference, Churchill and Roosevelt agreed that the main Anglo-American assault on Hitler's Europe, code-named Overlord, should be made in north-west France, accompanied by landings in the south of France, code-named Anvil.

By the time of the Cairo conference, the excitement of the summer of 1942 had vanished. At GHQ in Cairo officers spent as much time fighting each other for promotion as they did fighting the Italians and Germans, who had been driven out of North Africa in May 1943.

The SOE in Cairo

The Special Operations Executive (SOE) was a British agency established in July 1940 to gather information, carry out sabotage and support the Resistance in Axis-occupied countries. SOE operations in Greece and Yugoslavia were directed from its headquarters in Cairo, sometimes with spectacular success. In November 1942 180kg of plastic explosive from Cairo enabled British parachutists and Greek partisans to blow up the Gorgepotamos bridge on the Athens-Salonika railway, which carried vital supplies for Rommel who was then retreating westward from El Alamein.

As the war drew to a close, the population of Cairo counted the benefits it had brought. The Allies had spent huge sums of money in Egypt. The Egyptian government banked much of this in London, wiping out all its pre-war debt. Britain still owed Egypt £300 million for supplies, damages and compensation.

The wartime restriction on imports had boosted local industry, since the things that could no longer be bought abroad had to be made in Egypt. But with the coming of peace, Egypt's local industries found that they could not compete with the resumption of normal trade from abroad. This, combined with the dismantling of the Allied war machine, led to rising unemployment. In turn, this fuelled renewed anti-British feelings.

In March 1945, Egypt declared war on Germany to ensure a place in the new United Nations Organization (UNO). However, ordinary Egyptians felt that since 1939 they had been caught up in events over which they and their government had no real control. The war had been won but for nationalists the post-war struggle for an Egypt free from foreign control was just beginning.

Germany's spy in Cairo

The only German spy planted in Cairo during the war was an agent named John Eppler. Eppler was German-born but, since the First World War, he had lived in Alexandria, where his mother had married an Egyptian. Early in 1942 he crossed the desert with his radio operator and set himself up in Cairo on a luxurious houseboat. He then recruited an old girlfriend, a belly-dancer named Hekmet Fahmy, hoping that she would be able to tease information from amorous Allied officers. Eppler spent much of his time posing as a British officer, buying fellow-officers drinks in Cairo's bars and listening carefully to what they had to say. However, Eppler was more of a playboy than a master-spy. He was eventually caught by the British when the £5 notes he was spending so freely turned out to be forgeries. Eppler later claimed that the German secret service had not told him that the money it had given him was counterfeit. Eppler and his radio operator escaped execution because one of his Egyptian helpers had been a young Egyptian army officer, Anwar Sadat. To have shot Sadat - a popular nationalist - along with the two Germans would have provoked serious unrest in Egypt. All three were imprisoned.

John Eppler (left) and his captor British Major A.W. Sansom MBE, meet again some 18 years later.

Berlin

In Berlin on 3 September 1939 the usual cheering crowds were not there to salute Adolf Hitler as he drove to address the German parliament in the Kroll Opera House. Five hours earlier Britain had declared war and the Second World War had begun. The streets of Berlin were almost deserted that morning. Pedestrians huddled in groups, staring silently at the car which carried their Führer (or leader) in his field-grey uniform. There was no excitement at the news, only feelings of deep anxiety.

Sweeping German victories in France (summer 1940) and Russia (summer 1941) spared the inhabitants of Berlin many of the hardships of war. Goods of all kinds flooded in from the conquered territories: furs from Norway, Dutch dairy products, French silks and perfumes. In spite of rationing, food was in plentiful supply, supplemented by the clothing and foodstuffs sent home by soldiers in the occupied countries.

Until 1941, Berliners lived much as they had done before the war. The routines of work, school and annual holidays were not disturbed. German war industry marked time while the wives of soldiers away

Hitler and Berlin

Although it was Germany's capital, Berlin had never been a centre of Nazi strength. Before Hitler had come to power in January 1933 it had been a communist stronghold. Throughout the war Hitler spent little time in the city. Like a medieval king, he moved from one purpose-built headquarters to another. Their crumbling concrete hulks still litter Europe, from Soissons in France to Rastenburg in East Prussia (now part of Poland).

Relaxed pre-war days in a café in Berlin's famous Tiergarten park. By the end of the war the park was a no man's land of shell craters and wreckage-clogged lakes.

A German woman gives the finishing touches to an He111 bomber at the Heinkel works at Oranienburg in North Berlin.

at the war lived comfortably off their state allowances. It was not until 1941 that any attempt was made to direct women into the factories producing tanks, guns and aircraft. In crowded cafés and restaurants, silence regularly fell as the radio was turned up and a roll of drums and blast of trumpets heralded the announcement of the latest German victory.

The strain began to show in the winter of 1941. Germany was hit by its first food crisis. There was a shortage of farmworkers (called up to fight on the Eastern Front in Russia) and railway rolling stock (supplying the troops in Russia). This played havoc with the production and distribution of potatoes, the staple item in every German family's diet. Howard K. Smith, an American journalist based in Berlin wrote: *'People's faces are pale, unhealthily white as flour, except for the red rings around their eyes.'*

That winter, the German army was brought to a halt in the snows outside Moscow and then forced to retreat. For the first time in the war, large numbers of wounded soldiers began to appear in Berlin. Shortages started to bite. New clothing and footwear went straight to the armed forces, and civilians had to do without.

Wartime diet

In April 1942, potatoes were rationed. The film actress Hildegard Knef, who lived in Berlin through the war, later wrote about the wartime diet there. It consisted mainly of synthetic coffee (made with acorns), bread and margarine, and powdered egg that *'tasted faintly of glue'*.

In 1942, US and British bomber aircraft brought Germany's civilians into the front line. In November 1943, Berlin came under heavy attack. The chief of RAF Bomber Command, Air Chief Marshal Sir Arthur Harris, told Winston Churchill that he intended to *'wreck Berlin from end to end'*. He launched his bombing offensive, the Battle of Berlin, on 18 November when 440 four-engined Lancasters were despatched to bomb the Big City as the British air crews called Berlin.

The Battle of Berlin lasted four months. In 16 major attacks, Bomber Command dropped over 30,000 tonnes of bombs on the city. But Berlin proved too tough a nut for Harris and his bombers to crack. The Big City was too big (covering over 2,300km²), too well-defended and too far away from the bombers' bases in England to be 'wrecked'. Nevertheless, the bombers did terrible damage.

During the Battle of Berlin nearly a million women and children were evacuated from the city. The women who remained outnumbered able-bodied men in Berlin, most of whom were in the armed forces. At night schoolboys helped to operate anti-aircraft guns and searchlight batteries. Women were recruited into the fire-fighting service.

There was no mass panic in Berlin, but as the battle raged overhead it was clear to Berliners that Germany was losing the war. On the Eastern Front the Red Army was relentlessly rolling the Germans westward. By February 1945 the Red Army was only 100km from Berlin, threatening the city with overwhelming force. Retreating ahead of its advance, German refugees reached Berlin with terrible tales of Soviet cruelty. The Red Army was taking revenge for the millions of Soviet soldiers and civilians who had died at German hands. Many Germans bought poison capsules, preferring suicide to capture by the Russians.

Berlin's civilian population had fallen from its pre-war level of 4.3 million to about 2.7 million. Of these, about two million were women. The only males left in any numbers were children under 18 or men over 60.

A tide of refugees, fleeing before the Soviet advance, arrive in Berlin's Anhalter station during the last weeks of the war.

British and US bombers continued to pound Berlin by day and night. Three billion cubic feet of rubble and wreckage lay in the shattered streets, enough debris to build a mountain more than three hundred metres high. Every third house was either destroyed or made uninhabitable. Nevertheless, Berlin remained a functioning city. A strange kind of normality reigned in the ruins. People still struggled to work in the morning. Twelve thousand law officers remained on duty. The mail was still delivered. Daily newspapers were published. The telephones still worked. The Berlin Philharmonic Orchestra carried on to the end of its last wartime season of concerts. Even part of Berlin's famous zoo in the Tiergarten park was open.

Adolf Hitler had declared Berlin a fortress. But it was a fortress that existed only in Hitler's imagination. There was

Under the bombs

Brigitte Kirchstein was a child of six at the time of a heavy air raid on Berlin on 24/25 March 1944. Later she recalled: *'It was well into the next day when we came out of the shelter... Our homes were gone... We set off across the ruins. The most terrifying thing was that pieces of hot, glowing charcoal and timbers were falling down from the buildings we passed. We stumbled over the ruins until we reached the Spittelmarket railway station. There were no trains and people were sitting or lying on the lines and platforms... The next night we had to move on, still walking out of the ruined area until we reached a large building... where the bombed-out families were staying... poor Mother was very tired. Her skin had gone dark and grey in those last two days... She talked of Father with a hopeless expression on her face. He was missing in Russia.'[7]*

The shattered streets of Berlin at the end of the war. Incredibly, in April 1945, over 65 per cent of Berlin's factories still functioned but they were difficult to get to through streets choked with rubble. Everyone wanted to get to work on time because American bombers usually appeared over the city at 9 am – a bad time still to be on the street.

no defence plan and few troops to defend the city. Many of Berlin's defenders were the very young and the old, members of the *Volkssturm*, in which all men between the ages of 16 and 60 not in the armed forces but capable of bearing arms had to serve. A joke ran through Berlin that it would take the Soviets two hours and 15 minutes to break into the city: *'Two hours laughing their heads off, and 15 minutes demolishing the makeshift barricades erected by the Volkssturm.'*

After massive preparations, the Soviets launched their drive on Berlin on 16 April. Four days later, British and US planes made their last air raid on Berlin. Gas and electricity, sanitation and public transport – all functioning until this moment – finally collapsed. Street hydrants became the only source of water.

The Soviets smashed their way into the city, fighting against desperate resistance from street to street and house to house, scorching crumbling buildings with flame-throwers and blasting through the cellars. By 27 April the defenders of Berlin had been squeezed into a narrow east-west corridor about 4km wide and 16km long. The city was cut off from the outside world. Russian shells were plunging down on to the city centre, shaking the underground bunker in which Hitler had taken refuge. In the streets that as yet remained in German hands, fanatical SS squads hung deserters from street lamps or shot them on the spot. In their cellars Berliners hid and waited for the end.

Top: Last line of defence – an elderly member of the Volkssturm examines a rifle as big as himself. Above: Soviet troops race past a dead German in the centre of Berlin.

It came on the afternoon of 2 May. On 30 April Hitler had committed suicide. General Karl Weidling, the commander of what was left of Berlin's garrison, now isolated in three small pockets, surrendered to the Red Army.

Between 16 April and 2 May the Soviets had lost at least 100,000 troops in the taking of Berlin. German casualties are not known, but it is estimated that 200,000 soldiers and civilians died in the last battle of the war in the West. For months afterwards the stench of bodies lying under the rubble hung over Berlin as its population came to terms with total defeat.

Injured German soldiers receive treatment from the Red Cross near the Brandenburg Gate on 2 May 1945.

Leningrad

On 22 June 1941, Germany invaded the Soviet Union. In the south and north its armies advanced rapidly. Within weeks, millions of Soviet soldiers had been taken prisoner. By mid-September tanks of the German Army Group North were on the southern outskirts of the city of Leningrad (now returned to its original name of St. Petersburg), the old capital of the Tsars of Russia and the cradle of the Russian Revolution.

The Germans found their path blocked by fortifications built in a huge effort by half a million of Leningrad's citizens. Between the German tanks and the city were over 950km of earthworks, 650km of anti-tank ditches, 650km of barbed-wire entanglements and 5,000 concrete and wooden strongpoints. Leningrad was also protected from attack from the north by Lake Ladoga, a great expanse of water which stopped the German forces from surrounding the city.

The Germans knew it would be very costly to break into the city, but the people of Leningrad could not break out.

In the bleak Russian winter German troops advance into a Soviet village behind a tank of the 11th Panzer Division.

Red Army troops in action during the siege of Leningrad. Note their warm caps and winter camouflage smocks. The besieging Germans were not so well equipped to face the harshness of the Russian winter.

The Germans decided not to take Leningrad by storm. It was very well defended, and its capture would present them with the problem of feeding its population of three million throughout the harsh Russian winter. The German generals decided to let the people of Leningrad starve to death under siege. On 4 September German artillery began a heavy bombardment of the city. Air raids started many fires.

Inside Leningrad, hunger quickly became a more deadly enemy than German shells or bombs. At the beginning of September there was barely a month's supply of food in the city. To survive the winter, the people of Leningrad needed 1,000 tonnes of food a day. By the beginning of November they were receiving less than 500 tonnes a day, carried by rail to Tikhvin and then ferried across Lake Ladoga from Novaya Ladoga, where there was also a small airfield.

On 9 November, Tikhvin was captured by the Germans. Immediately the Soviets began to hack a 300km road through thick forest to bring supplies in a wide arc from Zaborye to Novaya Ladoga. The road was finished in a month and was crudely surfaced with branches. Exhausted volunteers shoved trucks through snowdrifts and up steep hills. It took most of the trucks over a week to make the 300km journey.

Living with rationing

Shortages of food and fuel in Leningrad turned life into a nightmare. The daily food ration grew ever smaller. By December 1941 rations had reached starvation level. Manual workers and important technical staff received 255g of bread and 49g of meat a day. Other workers, their dependants and children received only 130g of bread and 14g of meat, a fraction of the body's requirements. Often the meat was replaced by a foul jelly made of sheep's guts. The loss of a ration card was a sentence of death, since without a ration card it was impossible to get food. People ate cats, dogs and rats. There were rumours of cannibalism.

Fuel shortages meant that most offices and homes went without electric light and central heating. Once furniture and books had been burnt, there was no fuel for the stoves. Weakened by hunger, people had little resistance to disease. In December 1941, 52,000 Leningraders died, as many as normally died in a year. In January 1942, 148,000 died. The dead often lay where they fell in the street, frozen solid beneath drifts of snow. Some were buried in mass graves blasted in the frozen, rock-hard earth by high explosives. One woman recalled: *'You just stepped over corpses in the street and on the stairs. You simply stopped taking any notice… Some people went quite insane with hunger. And the practice of hiding the dead somewhere in the house and using their ration cards was very common.'*[8]

The cold which brought so much suffering also saved Leningrad. When Lake Ladoga froze solid, supplies were brought in by truck along an 'ice road'. On 9 December 1941, Soviet troops retook Tikhvin. By February 1942 up to 400 trucks a day were bringing in food and taking out civilians. Thousands trekked across the ice on foot, but many of them died before they reached the safety of shore. By the end of 1942, nearly a million people had been evacuated from Leningrad.

Leningrad's lifeline: A convoy of trucks rumbles over the 'ice road' across Lake Ladoga in the winter of 1941-2.

The fall of Tikhvin to the Germans between 9 November and 9 December forced the Soviets to create new supply routes to Leningrad.

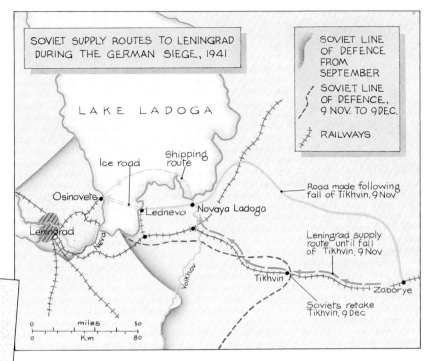

SOVIET SUPPLY ROUTES TO LENINGRAD DURING THE GERMAN SIEGE, 1941

SOVIET LINE OF DEFENCE FROM SEPTEMBER

SOVIET LINE OF DEFENCE, 9 NOV. TO 9 DEC.

RAILWAYS

LAKE LADOGA

Ice road

Shipping route

Osinovets

Lednevo

Novaya Ladoga

Leningrad

Neva

Volkhov

Road made following fall of Tikhvin, 9 Nov

Leningrad supply route until fall of Tikhvin, 9 Nov

Tikhvin

Zaborye

Soviets retake Tikhvin, 9 Dec

miles 50

Km 80

The threat of spring

Slowly the daily food ration crept upwards as supplies came in across Lake Ladoga, but the danger was not past. The spring thaw brought a threat of epidemics spreading from thousands of rotting corpses. An architect who survived the siege remembered: 'Many died in the spring when the worst was already over. The famine had peculiar physical effects on people... People had their feelings blunted and never seemed to weep at burials... It was all done in complete silence, without any displays of emotion. When things began to improve, the first signs were that women began to put rouge and lipstick on their pale, skinny faces.'⁹

Somehow, Leningrad survived. Throughout the siege, Leningrad's arms factories continued to turn out mortars, machine-guns and tanks. Starving and shivering in unheated factories, workers toiled for up to 15 hours a day. The communist youth organization, the *Komsomol*, organized 'everyday life' teams to help with housework, nurse the sick and care for thousands of children whose parents had died in the siege.

The population of Leningrad, now reduced by death and evacuation to 650,000 from the pre-war three million, was no longer in danger of starving. Indeed, their rations were now higher than in the rest of the Soviet Union. But many were still too weak to work or even move about.

Soviet troops opened up a direct land route to Leningrad in January 1943, but the siege continued for another year. At the end of January 1944 the Germans were finally driven away. Red, white and blue rockets streamed into the sky to celebrate the city's liberation. After 890 days it was free, but at a terrible cost. Over a million people had died during the siege.

Timeline

1929   **October 29th** Wall Street Crash, triggers Great Depression.
1931   April 14th Spain becomes a republic.
1933   January 30th Hitler appointed Chancellor of Germany. **August 2nd** Hitler becomes Führer (German dictator).
1935   October 2nd Italian troops invade Ethiopia.
1936   February Popular Front wins elections in Spain.
March 8th German troops enter Rhineland.
July 18th Rebellion by Army officers begins Spanish civil war. **November 1st** Italy and Germany sign Rome-Berlin Axis.
1937 July 7th Japan attacks China. **November 6th** Italy, Germany and Japan sign the Anti-Comintern Pact.
1938   March 12th Anschluss (union of Germany and Austria) declared: German troops occupy Austria.
August-September International confrontation over Hitler's demands for part of Czechoslovakia (the Sudetenland).
September 30th Munich Conference resolves Czech crisis.
October 12th German troops occupy Sudetenland.

1939 **March 12th** German forces occupy Czechoslovakia. **28th** Franco's forces capture Madrid: Spanish civil war ends. **31st** France and Britain guarantee Polish independence.
May 2nd Germany and Italy agree Pact of Steel alliance. **August 23rd** USSR-German non-aggression pact agreed. **September 1st** Germany invades western Poland. **3rd** France and Britain declare war on Germany. **17th** Soviet troops invade eastern Poland.

1940 **April 7th** Norway and Denmark attacked by Germany. **May 10th** German troops begin invasion of Netherlands, Belgium and Luxembourg. Churchill becomes British prime minister. **12th** Germany begins invasion of France.
June 10th Italy declares war on Britain and France. **14th** German forces capture Paris. **22nd** French sign armistice at Compiègne. Battle of Britain begins.
September 27th Germany, Italy and Japan sign the Tripartite Pact. **November 5th** Roosevelt re-elected US president. **14th** Coventry, England, levelled by German bombers.

1941 **March 11th** Lend-Lease Act signed. **April 17th** Germany starts invasion of Balkans and Greece. **June 22nd** Invasion of USSR by Germany (Operation Barbarossa) begins.
July US embargoes on oil and steel exports to Japan. **August 14th** Roosevelt and Churchill sign Atlantic Charter, agreeing war aims. **November** German forces halted outside Moscow.

December 7th Japan bombs US naval base at Pearl Harbor, Hawaii. Japan declares war on USA. **8th** USA and Britain declare war on Japan. **11th** Germany and Italy declare war on USA: USA declares war on them.

1942 **February 15th** Singapore captured by Japanese. **April 9th** US forces on Bataan Peninsula surrender. **May 6th** US forces on Corregidor surrender. **July** Battle of Stalingrad begins.
November 8th US and British troops land in North Africa. **11th** German forces enter Vichy France.

1943 **January 14-24th** Casablanca Conference agrees Allied war aim of unconditional enemy surrender. **February 2nd** German army at Stalingrad surrenders. **May 12th** War ends in North Africa. **July 10th** Allied forces land in Sicily.
26th Mussolini resigns. **September 3rd** Allies land in Italy. **8th** Italy surrenders. **10th** Nazi forces occupy Rome. **November 22-25th** Cairo Conference.
28th Tehran Conference opens.

1944 **March** Soviet troops re-enter Poland. **June 4th** Allied troops enter Rome.
6th D-day: Allied invasion of France begins. **July 20th** Hitler wounded in assassination attempt by German officers. **21st** Dumbarton Oaks conference lays down basis for United Nations. **August** Warsaw Uprising starts. **25th** Paris liberated. **October** Warsaw Uprising crushed. **6th** Soviet forces enter Hungary and Czechoslovakia. **20th** US forces enter Philippines.
November All-out US bombing of Japan begins.
December 16th German troops attack through Ardennes.

1945 **February 4th** Yalta conference. **April 1st** US forces occupy Okinawa.
12th Roosevelt dies: Truman US president. **20th** Soviet forces enter Berlin. **28th** Mussolini executed. **May 1st** Hitler's suicide announced in Berlin. **2nd** Berlin captured. **7th** Germany signs unconditional surrender.
June 26th UN formed. **July 17th** Potsdam conference opens. **August 6th** Atomic bomb dropped on Hiroshima. **8th** Atomic bomb dropped on Nagasaki.
September 2nd Japan signs surrender.

1946   **March 5th** Churchill's 'Iron Curtain' speech.
1947   **March 12th** Truman Doctrine outlined.
June 5th Marshall Plan put forward.
1948   **June 24th** USSR begins blockade of West Berlin (ends May12th 1949).

Glossary

Absenteeism   Staying away from work, or school, without an acceptable reason.

Allies   The USA, Britain and the other countries fighting the Axis powers in the Second World War.

Ambassador   A country's official representative abroad.

Axis   The powers allied to Germany in the Second World War; Italy (until 1943) and Japan.

Blitz   A term used in the Second World War to describe a sudden attack, especially from the air. It comes from the German word *Blitzkrieg*, or lightning war.

Communist   Believing in the political theory of Communism which says that the wealth produced by a country's industry and agriculture should benefit everyone in that country.

Concentration camps   Prison camps where, from the 1930s, the Germans imprisoned those they considered their enemies. They should not be confused with the death camps (see below).

Death camps   Prison camps of the Second World War (such as Treblinka in Poland) to which the Germans sent prisoners to be murdered.

Deportation   Forced removal to another country.

Dry dock   Enclosed dock from which the water is emptied to enable repairs to be made to the hulls of ships.

Exiled   Being expelled from one's native country.

Ghetto   A part of a city to which a minority population, especially Jewish, is confined.

Gold Rush   In 19th-century America there were successive Gold Rushes in which miners flooded into areas of the American West where deposits of gold had been discovered.

Greater East Asia Co-Prosperity Sphere   A Japanese propaganda term which was intended to convey to the people of colonial territories conquered by Japan that Japanese rule would bring great benefits. In fact Japanese rule was at least as harsh as that of the colonial powers.

Incendiary bomb   A bomb, usually dropped in clusters, which is designed to set fire to buildings rather than blow them apart.

Internment   The act of confining people within one country or one place.

Luftwaffe   The German air force.

Merchant ships   Trading ships.

Nominally   In name only.

Persecution   Ill-treatment of a person or people especially because of their political or religious beliefs.

Prefabricated steel   Steel that has been shaped into sections ready for putting together at another site to make, for example, ships and aircraft.

Radar   A system using pulses of radio energy to detect the approach of ships or aircraft.

Rationing   A system which controlled the amount of essential goods - food, fuel, clothing etc - available to civilians. This freed industry to concentrate on the production of war material and also ensured a fair share of the basics of life for everyone.

Red Army   The army of the former USSR.

Resistance   An organization of people fighting against the occupation of their country.

SS   Abbreviation for Shutzstaffeln (Protection Squads). Originally Hitler's bodyguard, the SS became very powerful and brutally imposed Hitler's will throughout Europe.

Synagogue   Jewish place of worship.

Third Reich   The Nazi empire from 1933 to 1945.

Tinder-box   A box containing things used to make a fire (tinder is a dry material such as wood which readily catches fire).

War Bonds   A US government scheme which encouraged people to give money to the war effort by buying savings certificates issued by the government.

Books to read

Blitzkrieg Peter Chrisp (Wayland, 1990)

Wayland's Home Front series, especially *The Blitz* by Fiona Reynoldson (1990); deals only with Britain

My Childhood in Nazi Germany Elsbeth Emmerich (Wayland, 1991); a record of life in Dusseldorf during the Second World War

Resistance Movements Conrad Stein (Franklin Watts, 1989)

The Second World War Charles Messenger (edited by Dr John Pimlott, Franklin Watts, 1986)

Sources of quotations
1, 1a, 2 and **3** *Valley of Darkness: The Japanese People and World War II,* Thomas R. Havens (Norton, 1978). **4** *Living through the Blitz,* Tom Harrison (Collins, 1976). **5** *The Making of London: London at War 1939-45,* Joanna Mack and Steve Humphries (Sidgwick & Jackson, 1985). **6** *Winter in the Morning: A Young Girl's Life in the Ghetto and Beyond,* Janina Bauman (Virago, 1986). **7** *The Berlin Raids,* Martin Middlebrook (Penguin, 1988). **8** and **9** *Russia at War,* Alexander Werth (Barrie & Rockliff, 1964).

Films

There are also some interesting films about cities during the Second World War, though historical accuracy varies enormously:

The Bells Go Down (1943); about the Blitz

Casablanca (1943)

Fires were Started (1943); action-documentary about the Blitz

Foxhole in Cairo (1961); about John Eppler, but not historically accurate

Germany, Year Zero (1947); about Berlin after the War, and shot in the ruins of the city

Kanal (1956); an excellent film about the Warsaw uprising

Swing Shift (1984); Goldie Hawn plays Rosie the Riveter opposite Kurt Russell

Index

*Numbers in **bold** show text accompanied by a picture or map.*